PRESENTED TO

Stories for a Mom's Heart

COMPILED *by* ALICE GRAY
ARTWORK *by* PAULA VAUGHAN

MULTNOMAH GIFTS™

Multnomah®Publishers *Sisters, Oregon*

Stories for a Mom's Heart

© 2000, 2002 by Multnomah Publishers, Inc.
published by Multnomah Publishers, Inc.
P.O. Box 1720, Sisters, Oregon 97759

ISBN 1-57673-917-1

Other stories in the *Stories for the Heart* Collection:
Stories for the Woman's Heart
Stories for a Cheerful Heart

Artwork by Paula Vaughan is reproduced with permission from Newmark Publishing USA.
For prints of the artwork, please contact:
Newmark Publishing USA
11700 Commonwealth Drive
Louisville, Kentucky 40299
1-800-866-5566
Designed by Koechel Peterson & Associates, Minneapolis, Minnesota

Multnomah Publishers, Inc.®, has made every effort to trace the ownership of all poems and quotes.
In the event of a question arising from the use of a poem or quote, we regret any error made and will be
pleased to make the necessary correction in future editions of this book.

Please see the acknowledgments at the back of the book for complete attributions for this material.

Scripture quotations are taken from *The Holy Bible*, New International Version © (1973, 1984) by International Bible
Society, used by permission of Zondervan Publishing House; *The Living Bible* (TLB) © (1971).
Used by permission of Tyndale House Publishers, Inc.

Multnomah is a trademark of Multnomah Publishers, Inc., and is registered in the U.S. Patent and Trademark Office.
The colophon is a trademark of Multnomah Publishers, Inc.

Printed in China

02 03 04 05 06 07 08—10 9 8 7 6 5 4 3 2

www.multnomahgifts.com

TABLE OF CONTENTS

I Found You There

KATHI KINGMA

I held on to your hand across streets, over hills, through the valleys. Though the wind blew, though I tripped, you never let me fall. Sometimes I didn't look all the way up to see your face, but I saw your hand. It was twice as big as mine. I tried to take big steps like you, to be like you. I still had to take two for each of yours. When my legs got tired, you carried me. It was fun to see everything from up high where I didn't have to try so hard to keep up. I always felt safe with my mom. As long as you were there, I know things would be okay. When I was scared, I reached for your hand and found you there.

When I got older, I wanted to walk more on my own. I learned to navigate the path of life, over hills and through the valleys.

I glimpsed at freedom and independence. You still walked beside me and helped me get up when I fell.

Now I am grown up. My stride equals yours. I look you in the eyes and I do not tire as we walk. But you have changed. You are still there as support, as counsel, as unchanging love. Because of you, a little one will rush up to me someday. Full of adventure, she'll walk with me across streets, over hills and through valleys. She'll take steps trying to make them big like mine. She'll trip and I'll catch her. She'll reach up for my hand and find me there.

My mother planted

seeds of faith

and watered them

with love.

ALICE GRAY

A Mother's Letter to a Son Starting Kindergarten

REBECCA CHRISTIAN

Dear George,

When your big brother and your little dog and I walked you up to school today, you had no idea how I was feeling.

You were so excited; you had packed and unpacked the washable markers and safety scissors in your backpack a dozen times.

I am really going to miss those lazy mornings when we waved your brother and sister off to school. I'd settle in with my coffee and newspaper, handing you the comics to color while you watched Sesame Street.

Because you are my youngest, I had learned a few things by the time you came along. I found out that the

seemingly endless days of babyhood are gone like light-ning. I blinked, and your older siblings were setting off for school as eagerly as you did this morning.

I was one of the lucky ones; I could choose whether to work or not. By the time it was your turn, the glitter-ing prizes of career advancement and a double income had lost their luster. A splash in the puddles with you in your bright red boots or "just one more" rereading of your favorite book, *Frog and Toad Are Friends*, meant more.

You didn't go to preschool and I'm not exactly Maria Montessori. I hope that doesn't hold you back. You learned numbers by helping me count the soda cans we returned to the store. (You could usually charm me into letting you pick out a treat with the money we got back.)

I'm not up on the Palmer method, but you do a fine job of writing your name on the sidewalk in chalk, in capitals to make it look more important. And somehow you caught on to the nuances of language. Just the other day, you asked me why I always call you "honey" when

we're reading stories and "bud" when you're helping with the chores. My explanation of the difference between a cuddly mood and a matey one seemed to satisfy you.

I have to admit that in my mind's eye, an image of myself while you're in school has developed. I see myself updating all the photo albums and starting that novel I always wanted to write. As the summer wound down and more frequent quarrels erupted between you and your siblings, I was looking forward to today.

And then this morning, I walked you up the steep hill to your classroom with a picture of the president on one wall and of Bambi on the opposite. You found the coat hook with your name above it right away, and you gave me one of your characteristically fierce, too tight hugs. This time you were ready to let go before I was.

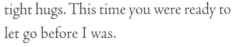

Maybe someday you will deliver a kindergartner with your own wide-set eyes and sudden grin to the first day of school. When you turn at the door to wave good-bye, he or she will be too deep in conversation with a new friend to notice. Even as you smile, you'll feel something warm on your cheek…

And then, you'll know.

Love, Mom

A mother's heart

is the child's

schoolroom.

HENRY WARD BEECHER

Twice Blessed

KATHRYN LAY

On the day my husband and I learned of our imminent adoption of our nine-month-old daughter, we joyously took our closest friends out to dinner in celebration.

While we laughed and talked at the restaurant, telling them of what we knew about our soon-to-arrive and much-prayed-for daughter, I became aware that the older couple in the booth behind us laughed as we did and nodded knowingly as we voiced our excitement and nervousness.

After ten years of infertility, of prayers, and eight months of parenting classes and paperwork and home studies—we were full of joy at the good news. It bubbled over as we talked and planned in the restaurant.

When the couple behind us left their booth, they paused at our table.

"Congratulations," the woman said, patting my shoulder.

"Thank you," I said, grateful that they weren't angry at our loudness.

She leaned closer and said, "I have several children of my own. I have a granddaughter who was adopted by someone not long ago. I've never seen her. Hearing your excitement, I feel in my heart that somewhere she is loved and well taken care of by a family like you."

Patting my shoulder once more, she whispered, "I'll pray for you and your baby."

At a time when we were blessed and overflowing with joy, God put us in a place where we could be a blessing and comfort to another. I pray for that grandmother, that God will continue to give her peace and comfort for the granddaughter she wonders about. And I know that my husband and I were in her prayers that night.

"For I know the plans I have

for you," declares the LORD,

"plans to prosper you

and not to harm you,

plans to give you

hope and a future."

JEREMIAH 29:11

This Is a Home
Where Children Live

JUDITH BOND

You may not find things all in place,

Friend, when you enter here.

But we're a home where children live,

We hold them very dear.

And you may find small fingerprints

And smudges on the wall.

When the kids are gone, we'll clean them up,

Right now we're playing ball.

For there's one thing of which we're sure,

These children are on loan.

One day they're always underfoot,

Next thing you know, they're gone.

That's when we'll have a well-kept house,

When they're off on their own.

Right now, this is where children live,

a loved and lived-in home.

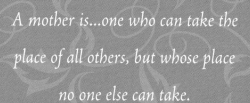

A mother is...one who can take the place of all others, but whose place no one else can take.

GASPARD MERMILLOD

Growing Pains

EDWINA PATTERSON

Amanda flounced into the house and plopped down on the couch. Her backpack came unbuckled and spilled its contents onto the floor. As she bent to pick them up, her pouty face and misty eyes immediately let me know something was wrong. Casually I asked, "What's going on?"

Her voice trembled as she poured out her feelings. I learned there was a new girl in school, and she was tall, blond, and beautiful. Both girls and boys were vying for her attention. They all liked her and wanted to be her new best friend. Amanda felt left out, awkward, and ugly.

Wrapping my arms around my child, I remembered how difficult and confusing the teenage years were. Growth spurts, body changes, emotions running up and down, and discovering the value of true friendships are enough to bewilder anyone. Trying to console her, I held her close, patted her back, and began to pray.

Oh Lord, as my child goes through the day, may she remember she's not alone. You are always with her…sitting in the cafeteria, hurrying down the hall, playing in the gym, and walking home.

Remind her you are the best friend she'll ever have. Your friendship isn't fickle. It doesn't change like the latest fad—here today and gone tomorrow. You are trustworthy and faithful. Not only do you know her innermost feelings and desires, but you continue to be her friend in spite of them.

May Amanda understand how much you love her. She's special to you. You created her and knit her together in my womb. There are no surprises to you. You knew she'd have dark, curly hair and big brown eyes. You knew she'd be a head shorter than everyone else her age, for you planned her stature.

You gave her this precious, sensitive heart full of feelings and love of life. May we both remember you have a plan for her life, and you're working on that plan now.

You're growing and stretching her with each new experience. Her encounters with disappointments and joys will fill her with wisdom and understanding for the heartaches and pain of others. Hold her impressionable heart gently and keep it responsive to you. As she learns to look beyond herself, may she see the needs of others through your eyes.

Help me to be the mom she needs. May household responsibilities and my own agenda not keep me so busy that I fail to notice her silent cries for help. As she observes my life, may she see a mom who loves and trusts you. May she not focus on my mistakes and failures, but only see the joy of your forgiveness. May my responses point her to you.

Reveal to me where you're working in her life and keep me alert to do my part in getting her ready to accomplish your plan. Fill me with wisdom as I guide her. May she face each day with confidence, knowing I am faithfully praying for her. In Jesus' name, amen.

Breakfast with
the Polar Bears

ALLISON HARMS

went to college when my son went to kindergarten. I had more homework than he did, but we shared the field trips—I chaperoned his class to the fire station and the farm and he joined my class for a couple of fossil hunts and glacier hikes. Once, for one of my biology classes, I was required to visit the zoo on my own sometime during the fall term. I put it off for weeks, waiting for Indian summer, busy with our new back-to-school schedules. Finally I realized that the end of the term was approaching and I hadn't completed the assignment. I chose a day for the zoo excursion. Of course my son came along too.

It wasn't a typical day at the zoo. The late fall, too early

winter weather kept it deserted except for my son and me. Even the animals seemed scarce. Clouds closed down the sky and spat rain that felt like ice needles. Damp gusts eddied around our legs, catching up shredded leaves, paper bags, candy wrappers, and peanut shells in a whirlpool of compost at the corner of the reptile house. Only a few eerie fluorescent lights glowed inside. We walked on. The fountains were drained, the garden beds left desolate, the boulevards empty. Ducks huddled together on the lee side of the lake, heads tucked under their wings. Tiny waves smacked the shore. As we walked, the wind filled then flattened our coats against our bodies.

Our footfalls on the paved walk alerted the gazelles at their grazing. A herd of sharp heads, ears, and horns poised like a ballet troupe on tiptoe as we passed. In the distance, we heard the elephant's bugle. The lion's amber eyes followed us; his tufted tail flicked once against the floor. The surface of the hippopotamus's pool winked and the matron lifted her bulbous snout and blinked her

liquid eye. The giraffe cocked his head and stared gravely.

We stopped to watch the polar bears. They marched with cool, lumbering strides but their gait was comically bow-legged and pigeon-toed. They had overgrown puppies' paws fringed with curved, black claws. Muzzles up, they sniffed the air, swinging their too small, bullet heads from side to side and snorting dragon curls of steam against the cement sky. The scent of snow was as comforting to them as a sunbath for a house cat.

Their keeper came around the corner wearing rubber boots and swinging two red buckets. At their first sight of him, the bears began to plunge into the pool with the rumbling chaos of boulders in an avalanche. They clambered out again, water streaming from their bodies like snowmelt from the mountains.

The keeper walked over to where my son and I stood.

"Good morning," we said to each other. I asked him what was in the buckets.

"Mackerel and watermelon."

"Is that what bears eat for breakfast?" my son asked.

"Yep," the keeper answered. Then bending down to my son's height, he said, "Like to help me feed the bears?"

"Wow! Can I, Mom?"

And so we did, tossing dark wedges of fish and mottled melon rinds into winter's first breath of snow.

Too soon it was time to leave. My son was tired so I carried him in my arms, his hood pulled over his ears, his face pressed into my shoulder. I smiled to myself as I thought of how often the "have tos" in my life turned into "get tos": I had to go to the zoo; I got to spend the day with my son and feed breakfast to the polar bears. Doing what's right has rewards of its own. But I could remember so many times when I'd fulfilled an obligation or followed through on a promise even when it cost me to keep it, and something new had opened up for me: a relationship, a skill, an unforgettable moment. And even on the blustery November day, I knew that the memory of our simple, unexpected experience—breakfast with the polar bears—would warm us deep down inside every time we remembered it.

*Mother love is that
divine gift which comforts,
purifies, and strengthens
all who seek it.*

LOUISA MAY ALCOTT

Mother's Legacy

I shall never forget my mother, for it was she who planted

and nurtured the first seeds of good within me.

She opened my heart to the impressions of nature;

she awakened my understanding

and extended my horizon, and

her precepts exerted an everlasting influence

upon the course of my life.

IMMANUEL KANT

Alone Time for Mom

CRYSTAL KIRGISS

*A*ll I needed this morning was a half-hour alone, thirty minutes of peace and quiet to help preserve my sanity. No mom-do-this, mom-I-need-that, mom-he-hit-me, mom-I-spilled-juice-on-the-couch.

Just me, a hot Calgon bath, and nothingness.

I shouldn't dream so big.

After getting the two oldest off to school, I settled the youngest in front of Barney and said, "Honey, listen closely. Your mommy is going to crack. She's losing her marbles. She's teetering on the edge of permanent personality damage. This is because she has children. Are you following me so far?"

He nodded absently while singing, "Barney is a dinosaur in our imagination…."

"Good. Now, if you want to be a good little boy, you'll

sit right here and watch Barney while Mommy takes a nice, hot, quiet, peaceful, take-me-away bath. I don't want you to bother me. I want you to leave me alone. For thirty minutes, I don't want to see you or hear you. Got it?"

Nod.

"Good morning, boys and girls…" I heard the purple wonder say.

I headed to the bathroom with my fingers crossed.

I watched the water fill the tub. I watched the mirror and window steam up. I watched the water turn blue from my bath beads. I got in.

I heard a knock on the door.

"Mom? Mom? Are you in there, Mom?!"

I learned long ago that ignoring my children does not make them go away.

"Yes, I'm in here. What do you want?"

There was a long pause while the child tried to decide what he wanted.

"Um…can I have a snack?"

"You just had breakfast! Can't you wait a few minutes?"

"No, I'm dying! I need a snack right now!"

"Fine. You can have a box of raisins."

I heard him pad off to the kitchen, listened as he pushed chairs and stools around trying to reach the raisin shelf, felt the floor vibrate when he jumped off the counter, and heard him run back to the TV room.

"Hi, Susie! Can you tell me what color the grass is…?"

Knock, knock, knock.

"Mom? Mom? Are you in there, Mom?!"

Sigh. "Yes, I'm still in here. What do you need now?"

Pause. "Um…I need to take a bath, too."

Right.

"Honey, can't you wait until I'm done?"

The door opened just a crack.

"No, I really need to take one now. I'm dirty."

"You're always dirty! Since when do you care?"

The door opened all the way.

"I really need to take a bath, Mom."

"No, you don't. Go away."

He stood in the middle of the bathroom and started taking off his pajamas.

"I'll just get in with you and take a bath, too."

"No! You will not get in with me and take a bath! I want to take my own bath! I want you to go away and leave me alone!" I began to sound like the three-year-old with whom I was arguing.

He climbed onto the edge of the tub, balancing carefully, and said, "I'll just get in with you, okay, Mom?"

I started to shriek, "No! That is not okay! I want my own bath, all by myself! I don't want to share! I want to be alone!"

He thought for a moment and said, "Okay. I'll just sit here and you can read me a book. I won't get in, Mom, until you're done." He flashed me a knock-down charming smile.

So I spent my morning alone-time reading *One Fish, Two Fish* to a naked three-year-old who sat on the edge of the tub with his chin resting on his knees, arms wrapped around his bent legs, slight smile on his face.

Why fight it? It won't be long before I have all the alone-time I want. And then I'll probably feel bad about not having any more together-time.

A MOTHER'S SACRIFICE

I have been told that my mother, when she surmised from the face of the physician that her life and that of her child could not both be saved, begged him to spare the child....

So through these many years of mine, I have seldom thanked God for His mercies without thanking Him for my mother.

JAMES M. LUDLOW

Love Letters to My Unborn Child

JUDITH HAYES

It was a balmy summer day in late July. I had been feeling rather queasy and nauseated, so I decided to see my doctor.

"Mrs. Hayes, I'm happy to tell you that you are ten weeks pregnant," my doctor announced. I couldn't believe my ears. It was a dream come true.

My husband and I were young and had been married for only a year. We were working hard to build a happy life together. The news that we were expecting a baby was exciting and scary.

In my youthful enthusiasm I decided to write "love letters" to our baby to express my feelings of expectancy and joy. Little did I know just how valuable those love letters would be in years to come.

August 1971: Oh, my darling baby, can you feel the love I have for you while you are so small and living in the quiet world inside my body? Your daddy and I want the world to be perfect for you with no hate, no wars, no pollution. I can't wait to hold you in my arms in just six months! I love you, and Daddy loves you but he can't feel you yet.

September 1971: I am four months pregnant and am feeling better. I can tell you are growing, and I hope you are well and comfortable. I've been taking vitamins and eating healthy foods for you. Thank goodness my morning sickness is gone. I think about you all the time.

October 1971: Oh, these melancholy moods. I cry so often over so little. Sometimes I feel very alone, and then I remember you are growing inside of me. I feel you stirring, now tumbling and turning and pushing. It's never the same. Your movements always bring me so much joy!

November 1971: I am feeling much better now that my fatigue and nausea have passed. The intense heat of summer is over. The weather is lovely, crisp and breezy.

I feel your movements often now. Constant punching and kicking. What elation to know you are alive and well. Last week Daddy and I heard your strong heartbeat at the doctor's office.

February 2, 1972 at 11:06 P.M.: You were born! We named you Sasha. It was a long, hard twenty-two-hour labor, and your daddy helped me relax and stay calm. We are so happy to see you, to hold you, and to greet you. Welcome, our firstborn child. We love you so much!

Sasha was soon one year old and cautiously toddling all over the house. Then she was riding ponies and swinging in the sunshine at the park. Our little blue-eyed beauty entered kindergarten and grew into a bright and strong-willed little girl. The years passed so quickly that my husband and I joked that we put our five-year-old daughter to bed one night and she woke up the next morning as a teenager.

Those few years of adolescence and rebellion were not easy. There were times my beautiful yet angry teenager

would dig her feet into the ground and yell. "You never loved me! You don't care about me or want me to be happy!"

Her harsh words cut at my heart. What could I have done wrong?

After one of my daughter's angry outbursts, I suddenly remembered the little box of love letters tucked away in my bedroom closet. I found them and quietly placed them on her bed, hoping she would read them. A few days later, she appeared before me with tears in her eyes.

"Mom, I never knew just how much you truly loved me—even before I was born!" she said. "How could you love me without knowing me? You loved me unconditionally!" That very precious moment became a bond of unity that still exists between us today. Those dusty old love letters melted away the anger and rebellion she had been feeling.

It was when

I had my first child

that I understood how much

my mother loved me.

AUTHOR UNKNOWN

To My Grown-Up Son

AUTHOR UNKNOWN

My hands were busy through the day;
I didn't have much time to play
The little games you asked me to—
I didn't have much time for you.

I'd wash your clothes, I'd sew and cook;
But when you'd bring your picture book
And ask me please to share your fun,
I'd say: "A little later, son."
I'd tuck you in all safe at night,
And hear your prayers, turn out the light,
Then tip-toe softly to the door...
I wish I'd stayed a minute more.
For life is short, the years rush past...
A little boy grows up so fast.
No longer is he at your side,
His precious secrets to confide.
The picture books are put away;
There are no longer games to play.
No good-night kiss, no prayers to hear—
That all belongs to yesteryear.
My hands, once busy, now are still.
The days are long and hard to fill.
I wish I could go back and do
The little things you asked me to.

Seeing Each Other in a Different Light

SUSAN MANEGOLD

When my daughters were little, we loved to spend time together talking or watching TV. But by the time Lauren and Carly were teens, they preferred being in their own rooms, talking on the phone or listening to music, to being with me—or even each other.

I knew it was just a part of their growing up, but while I wanted my daughters to be independent, I also wanted them to be close, and a part of me missed the days when we'd all curl up on the couch with a bowl of popcorn.

Then one windy night while their dad was working, the lights went out. "Cool!" I heard Carly, thirteen, call from her room.

"I hate this!" Lauren, eighteen, cried.

Grabbing candles and a flashlight, I headed for the girls' rooms. Lauren's was already filled with the cozy glow of candlelight, so Carly and I filed in, and soon we were all snuggled on Lauren's bed.

Carly was excited, but Lauren pouted when Carly suggested, "Let's tell stories." As Carly began to talk about school and her friends, however, Lauren's pout disappeared. She snuggled closer to Carly, and soon they were giggling just like they had when they were younger.

I could tell from the sparkle in Carly's eyes that she knew the darkness had brought us a gift, but I wondered if Lauren felt the same way. Suddenly, Lauren's phone rang. "Yeah, our power is out too," she told her friend. "But I'll have to call you back. I'm hanging out with my mom and my sister."

She knows it too! I thought. And after she hung up, she offered, "Let's sing songs." Tears filled my eyes.

A short while later, the power came back on. "Oh no!" the girls groaned. But since then, we've all felt closer. We hug more, and the girls don't tease each other as much. Some nights we just sit and talk. The power outage didn't just leave us in the dark; it gave us the opportunity to see each other in a different light.

No language can express the power

and beauty and heroism and majesty

of a mother's love.

E. H. CHAPIN

She's Seventeen

GLORIA GAITHER

The first day of school didn't start until one o'clock, so there was plenty of time for breakfast at McDonald's and shopping for the supplies that had been listed in the *Times-Tribune* the Wednesday before. You reminded us to go to McDonald's for breakfast. "We've always gone there on the first day of school," you said. Something hard to label stirred inside me when you said it. Perhaps it was pride—pride that you still found joy in our crazy little tradition; or perhaps it was pleasure—pleasure in knowing that you still choose to be with our family when you have your "druthers." But there was a certain sadness, too, and I couldn't stop the knowing this was your last first day of school.

You came down the stairs that morning all neat and well-groomed, the healthy glow of your summer tan and

freckles still showing through your make-up, your sun-bleached hair carefully arranged. "Hi, Mom!" you said, and your grin showed your straight, white teeth. No more orthodontist appointments, I thought, and no more broken glasses to glue before school. Contacts and braces had sure been worth it.

"I've got to have my senior pictures taken tomorrow after school, Mom. Can I use the car?"

"As far as I know," I answered, then reminded you of your promise to take your sister to get her hair trimmed at three o'clock that afternoon. Your driver's license had come in handy, too.

By then Amy and Benjy were ready, and we all piled into the car and drove to McDonald's. As we ate, we talked about other first days—the first day of kinder-garten, their first day of junior high, and that scary first day in the big new high school. You all interrupted each other with stories of embarrassing moments, awards, friendships, and fright.

After we had eaten, we hurried to buy notebook paper and compasses before I dropped you all at school—first Amy and Benjy at the middle school, then you. "Bye, Mom," you said as you scooted across the seat. Then you stopped a moment and looked back over your shoulder. "And, Mom…thanks." It was the remnant of a kiss good-bye. It was the hesitancy of a little girl in ringlets beginning kindergarten. It was the anticipation of a young woman confident of her direction—these were all there in that gesture.

"I love you," was all I answered, but I had hoped that somehow you could hear with your heart the rest of the words that were going through my mind—words that told you how special you are to us; words that would let you know how rich your father and I have been because you came into our lives; words that tell you how much we believe in you, hope for you, pray for you, thank God for you. As the school doors closed behind you and you disappeared into the corridor, I wanted so to holler after

you: "Wait! We have so much yet to do. We've never been to Hawaii. We've never taken a cruise. That book of poetry we wrote together isn't published yet. And what about the day we were going to spend at the cabin just being still and reading? Or the writers' workshop we planned to attend together in Illinois? You can't go yet.… Wait!"

But I knew you couldn't wait, and that we could never keep you by calling a halt to your progress. You had promises to keep. And so, though I knew this was a last first, I also somehow knew that it was a first in a whole lifetime of new beginnings…and I rejoiced!

Nothing can compare in beauty,

and wonder, and admirableness,

and divinity itself, to the silent work

in obscure dwellings of faithful women

bringing their children to honor

and virtue and piety.

HENRY WARD BEECHER

Heartmade Valentine

EDWINA PATTERSON

"*I* can't! I can't! I can't!"

Those words and a very sad countenance tore at my heart as I entered Susie's room. She sat dejectedly in the midst of ribbon, glue, glitter, crayons, and red and white paper. I sat next to her on the floor and gathered her close to me.

"What's wrong, honey?"

"I can't make a heart for my Valentine. It comes out shaped wrong!"

I explained that sometimes cutting shapes is difficult for a five-year-old. I suggested I make a cardboard heart pattern. She could trace around it and follow the lines as she cut.

Busily we set to work. Susie carefully traced around

the pattern and cut out the outlined heart. Triumphantly, she held it up and proceeded to decorate it, scattering glitter and ribbon over the floor. I quietly left the room and continued with my other responsibilities.

Absorbed in her work, she didn't notice when I occasionally peeked into her room. There was a contentedness, a peace about her actions and soft melodies poured from her heart. Her songs warmed my soul and made my chores seem lighter.

When she finished, she proudly walked over to me and said, "Here, Mommy, this Valentine's for you."

My heart melted as I hugged her and prayed,

O Lord, how I love this child! She simply needed a pattern, a guide, to show her the way. Oh, Father, she needs a pattern for life, too. Reveal Susie's true needs to me and fill me with insight to know how to meet them.

May I be a godly example for her. In all my actions and words, may I point her to you, our pattern for life. May she see in me a mom who loves you, who listens to your instructions, and who willingly follows your directions. May she see my life filled with your peace because I trust you to be my daily guide.

Just as she lovingly offered her handmade Valentine to me, may she come to understand you lovingly offer your love to us in the form of your Son. May she realize Jesus Christ is your Valentine—sent from above—not wrapped in glitter and ribbons, but wrapped in perfect love. As I have reached out and joyously accepted her gift of love, may she open her heart to accept your gift of love. In Jesus' name, amen.

I remember my mother's prayers

and they have always followed me.

They have clung to me all my life.

ABRAHAM LINCOLN

Someday

CHARLES R. SWINDOLL

Someday when the kids are grown, things are going to be a lot different. The garage won't be full of bikes, electric train tracks on plywood, sawhorses surrounded by chunks of two-by-fours, nails, a hammer and saw, unfinished "experimental projects," and the rabbit cage. I'll be able to park both cars neatly in just the right places, and never again stumble over skateboards, a pile of papers (saved for the school fund drive), or the bag of rabbit food—now split and spilled.

Someday when the kids are grown, the kitchen will be incredibly neat. The sink will be free of sticky dishes, the garbage disposal won't get choked on rubber bands or paper cups, the refrigerator won't be clogged with nine bottles of milk, and we won't lose the tops to jelly jars, catsup bottles, the peanut butter, the margarine, or the

mustard. The water jar won't be put back empty, the ice trays won't be left out overnight, the blender won't stand for six hours coated with the remains of a midnight malt, and the honey will stay inside the container.

Someday when the kids are grown, my lovely wife will actually have time to get dressed leisurely. A long, hot bath (without three panic interruptions), time to do her nails (even toenails if she pleases!) without answering a dozen questions and reviewing spelling words, having had her hair done that afternoon without trying to squeeze it in between racing a sick dog to the vet and a trip to the orthodontist with a kid in a bad mood because she lost her headgear.

Someday when the kids are grown, the instrument called a "telephone" will actually be available. It won't look like it's growing from a teenager's ear. It will simply hang there… silently and amazingly available! It will be free of lipstick, human saliva, mayonnaise, corn chip crumbs, and toothpicks stuck in those little holes.

Someday when the kids are grown, I'll be able to see

through the car windows. Fingerprints, tongue licks, sneaker footprints and dog tracks (nobody knows how) will be conspicuous by their absence. The back seat won't be a disaster area, we won't sit on jacks or crayons anymore, the tank will not always be somewhere between empty and fumes, and (glory to God!) I won't have to clean up dog messes another time.

Someday when the kids are grown, we will return to normal conversations. You know, just plain American talk. "Gross" won't punctuate every sentence seven times. "Yuk!" will not be heard. "Hurry up, I gotta go!" will not accompany the banging of fists on the bathroom door. "It's my turn" won't call for a referee. And a magazine article will be read in full without interruption, then discussed at length without mom and dad having to hide in the attic to finish the conversation.

Someday when the kids are grown, we won't run out of toilet tissue. My wife won't lose her keys. We won't forget to shut the refrigerator door. I won't have to dream up

new ways of diverting attention from the gumball machine...or have to answer "Daddy, is it a sin that you're driving forty-seven in a thirty-mile-per-hour zone?"...or promise to kiss the rabbit good night...or wait up forever until they get home from dates...or have to take a number to get a word in at the supper table...or endure the pious pounding of one Keith Green just below the level of acute pain.

Yes, someday when the kids are grown, things are going to be a lot different. One by one they'll leave our nest, and the place will begin to resemble order and maybe even a touch of elegance. The clink of china and silver will be heard on occasion. The crackling of the fireplace will echo through the hallway. The phone will be strangely silent. The house will be quiet...and calm...and always clean...and empty...and we'll spend our time not looking forward to Someday but looking back to Yesterday. And thinking, "Maybe we can baby-sit the grandkids and get some life back in this place for a change!"

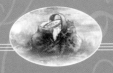

Before becoming a mother

I had a hundred theories

on how to bring up children.

Now I have seven children

and only one theory;

love them,

especially when they

least deserve it.

KATE SAMPERI

The Bobby Pins

LINDA GOODMAN

When I was seven years old, I overheard my mother tell one of her friends that the following day was to be her thirtieth birthday. Two things occurred to me when I heard that: one, I had never before realized that my mother had a birthday; and two, I could not recall her ever getting a birthday present.

Well, I could do something about that. I went into my bedroom, opened my piggy bank and took out all the money that was inside: five nickels. That represented five weeks' worth of my allowance. Then I walked to the little store around the corner from my house, and I told the proprietor, Mr. Sawyer, that I wanted to buy a birthday present for my mother.

He showed me everything in his store that could be had for a quarter. There were several ceramic figurines. My

mother would have loved those, but she already had a house full of them and I was the one who had to dust them once a week. They definitely would not do. There were also some small boxes of candy. My mother was diabetic, so I knew they would not be appropriate.

The last thing Mr. Sawyer showed me was a package of bobby pins. My mother had beautiful long black hair, and twice a week she washed and pincurled it. When she took the pincurls down the next day, she looked just like a movie star with those long, dark curls cascading around her shoulders. So I decided those bobby pins would be the perfect gift for my mother. I gave Mr. Sawyer my five nickels, and he gave me the bobby pins.

I took the bobby pins home and wrapped them in a colorful sheet from the Sunday comics (there was no money left for wrapping paper). The next morning, I walked up to my mother and handed her that package and said, "Happy birthday, Momma!"

My mother sat there for a moment in stunned silence. Then, with tears in her eyes, she tore at that comic-strip wrapping. By the time she got to the bobby pins, she was sobbing.

"I'm sorry, Momma!" I apologized. "I didn't mean to make you cry. I just wanted you to have a happy birthday."

"Oh, honey, I am happy!" she told me. And I looked into her eyes, and I could see that she was smiling through her tears. "Why, do you know that this is the first birthday present that I have ever received in my entire life?" she exclaimed.

Then she kissed me on the cheek and said, "Thank you, honey." And she turned to my sister and said, "Lookee here! Linda got me a birthday present!" And she turned to my father and said, "Lookee here! Linda got me a birthday present!"

And then she went into the bathroom to wash her hair and pincurl it with her new bobby pins.

After she left the room, my father looked at me and

said, "Linda, when I was growing up, back on the frontier (my daddy always called his childhood home in the mountains of Virginia the frontier), we didn't set much store by giving birthday presents to adults. That was something done just for small young'uns. And your momma's family, they were so poor, they didn't even do that much. But seeing how happy you've made your momma today has made me rethink this whole birthday issue. What I'm trying to say, Linda, is I believe you have set a precedent here."

And I did set a precedent. After that, my mother was showered with birthday presents every year: from my sister, from my brothers, from my father and from me. And, of course, the older we children got, the more money we made, and the nicer presents she received. By the time I was twenty-five, I had given her a stereo, a color television, and a microwave oven (which she traded in for a vacuum cleaner).

For my mother's fiftieth birthday, my brothers and my sister and I pooled our resources and got her something spectacular: a ring set with a pearl surrounded by a cluster

of diamonds. And when my oldest brother handed that ring to her at the party that was given in her honor, she opened up the velvet gift box and peered at the ring inside. Then she smiled and turned the box around so that her guests could see her special gift, and she said, "Don't I have wonderful children?" Then she passed the ring around the room, and it was thrilling to hear the collective sigh that rippled through that room as the ring was passed from hand to hand.

After the guests were gone, I stayed to help clean up. I was doing the dishes in the kitchen when I overheard a conversation between my mother and father in the next room. "Well, Pauline," my father said, "that's a mighty pretty ring you've got there. I reckon that's about the best birthday present you've ever had."

My own eyes filled with tears when I heard her reply. "Ted," she said softly, "that's a might pretty ring and that's a fact. But the best birthday present I ever got? Well, that was a package of bobby pins."

Her children stand and bless her;

so does her husband.

He praises her with these words:

"There are many fine women

in the world, but you are

the best of them all!"

PROVERBS 31:28–29, TLB

Her Path of Love

CLARE DELONG

*L*ooking out through our kitchen window we can see a path from our porch through the grass to the property adjoining ours. That property belongs to my mother—that path also belongs to her.

Some time ago, I was involved in a near fatal car accident. With nine bones broken and other injuries, I needed constant care and my future recovery meant a possible stay in a rehabilitation center.

My husband decided a few days before my discharge to take me home. The doctor approved and the equipment that would be needed was shipped and set up in the spare bedroom. Wally and Mom had accepted the responsibility of caring for me twenty-four hours a day.

That's when her path began. It continued to be used every day. For the next two and a half months Mom

traveled that path in sunshine, rain, snow, and sleet, during the morning and afternoon hours, even sometimes in the middle of the night.

I call it her path of love. The things she did for me at that time are as many as the stars in the sky. She cared for me as only a mother could. Her love, tenderness, and gentleness shown to me will never be forgotten. Eighteen months later the path remains—a visible sign of a mother's love.

Duty makes us do things well,

but love makes us do things beautifully.

PHILLIPS BROOKS

Now we behold two persons joined Both to be one

Got a Minute?

DAVID JEREMIAH

A mother who had just finished reading a book on parenting…was convicted about some of the things she had been failing to do as a parent. Feeling this conviction, she went upstairs to talk to her son. When she got upstairs, all she could hear coming from her boy's room was the loud sound of his drums. She had a message she wanted to deliver, but when she knocked on the door, she got cold feet.

"Got a minute?" she said, as her son answered her knock.

"Mom, you know I always have a minute for you," said the boy.

"You know, son, I…I…I just love the way you play the drums."

He said, "You do? Well, thanks, Mom!"

She got up and started back downstairs. Halfway down, she realized that she had not conveyed the message she had intended so back she went to his door and once again knocked. "It's Mom again! Do you have another minute?" she said.

He said, "Mom, like I told you before, I always have a minute for you."

She went over and sat on the bed. "When I was here before I had something I wanted to tell you and I didn't get it said. What I really meant to say was…your dad and I…we just really think you're great."

He said, "You and Dad?"

She said, "Yes, your Dad and I."

"Okay, Mom. Thanks a lot."

She left and was once again halfway down the stairs when she realized she had gotten closer to the message she intended but had still not told her boy that she loved him. So up the stairs again and back to the door again, and this time he heard her coming. Before she

could ask he shouted, "Yeah, I have a minute!"

Mom sat down on the bed once more. "You know, son, I've tried this twice now and haven't gotten it out. What I really came up here to tell you is this. I love you. I love you with all my heart. Not Dad and I love you, but I love you."

He said, "Mom, that's great. I love you, too!" He gave her a great big hug.

She started out of the room and was back at the head of the stairs when her son stuck his head out of his room and said, "Mom, do you have a minute?"

She laughed and said, "Sure."

"Mom," he said, "did you just come back from a seminar?"

No man is poor

who has a

godly mother.

ABRAHAM LINCOLN

Love's Sacrifice

KATHI KINGMA

Going to an affluent high school wasn't easy. I watched with envy as many of the "rich" kids drove their parents' sports cars and bragged about where they bought their designer clothes. I knew there was never a chance for me to compete with their wealthy status, but I also knew that it was a near crime if you wore the same outfit twice in the same month.

Coming from a family of five with a tight budget allowed us little hope for style. That didn't stop me from badgering my parents that I needed more fashionable clothes. My mother would frown at me. "Do you need them?"

"Yes," I would say adamantly. "I need them."

So shopping we would go. My mom waited outside the dressing room while I tried on the nicest clothes we could afford. I can recall several of these "necessity trips."

Mom always went without complaining, never trying anything on for herself, though she'd look.

One day, when I was at home, I tried on one of my new outfits and modeled it in front of my parents' full-length mirror. As I was deciding what shoes looked best with the outfit, my eyes wandered to their closet, which was partially open. What I saw brought tears to my eyes. Three shirts hung on my mom's side of the closet. Three shirts that she'd worn endlessly and were old and faded. I pulled open the closet farther to see a few work shirts of my dad's that he'd worn for years. It had been ages since they bought anything for themselves, though their need was greater than mine.

That moment opened my eyes to see the sacrifices my parents had made over the years, sacrifices that showed me their love more powerfully than any words they could have said.

Strength of character
is learned at work,
but beauty of character
is learned at home.

HENRY DRUMMOND

Christmas Lost and Found

SHIRLEY BARKDALE

We called him our Christmas Boy, because he came to us during that season of joy, when he was just six days old. Already his eyes twinkled more brightly than the lights on his first tree.

Later, as our family expanded, he made it clear that only he had the expertise to select and decorate the tree each year. He rushed the season, starting his gift list before we'd even finished the Thanksgiving turkey. He pressed us into singing carols, our croaky voices sounding more froglike than ever compared to his perfect pitch. He stirred us up, led us through a round of merry chaos.

Then, on his twenty-fourth Christmas, he left us as unexpectedly as he had come. A car accident on an icy Denver street, on his way home to his young wife and infant daughter. But first he had stopped by the

family home to decorate our tree, a ritual he had never abandoned.

Without his invincible Yuletide spirit, we were like poorly trained dancers, unable to perform after the music had stopped. In our grief, his father and I sold our home, where memories clung to every room. We moved to California, leaving behind our support system of friends and church. All the wrong moves.

It seemed I had come full circle, back to those early years when there had been just my parents and me. Christmas had always been a quiet, hurried affair, unlike the celebrations at my friends' homes, which were lively and peopled with rollicking relatives. I vowed then that someday I'd marry and have six children, and that at Christmas my house would vibrate with energy and love.

I found the man who shared my dream, but we had not reckoned on the surprise of infertility. Undaunted, we applied for adoption, ignoring gloomy prophecies that an adopted child would not be the same as "our own flesh and

blood." Even then, hope did not run high; the waiting list was long. But against all odds, within a year he arrived and was ours. Then nature surprised us again, and in rapid succession we added two biological children to the family. Not as many as we had hoped for, but compared to my quiet childhood, three made an entirely satisfactory crowd.

Those friends were right about adopted children not being the same. He wasn't the least like the rest of us. Through his own unique heredity, he brought color into our lives with his gift of music, his irrepressible good cheer, his bossy wit. He made us look and behave better than we were.

In the sixteen years that followed his death, time added chapters to our lives. His widow remarried and had a son; his daughter graduated from high school. His brother married and began his own Christmas traditions in another state. His sister, an artist, seemed fulfilled by her career. His father and I grew old enough to retire, and in Christmas of 1987 we decided to return to Denver. The call home was

unclear; we knew only that we yearned for some indefinable connection, for something lost that had to be retrieved before time ran out.

We slid into Denver on the tail end of a blizzard. Blocked highways forced us through the city, past the Civic Center, ablaze with thousands of lights—a scene I was not ready to face. This same trek had been one of our Christmas Boy's favorite holiday traditions. He had been relentless in his insistence that we all pile into the car, its windows fogged over with our warm breath, its tires fighting for a grip in ice.

I looked away from the lights and fixed my gaze on the distant Rockies, where he had loved to go barreling up the mountainside in search of the perfect tree. Now in the foothills there was his grave—a grave I could not bear to visit.

Once we were settled in the small, boxy house, so different from the family home where we had orchestrated our lives, we hunkered down like two barn swallows

who had missed the last migration south. While I stood staring toward the snowcapped mountains one day, I heard the sudden screech of car brakes, then the impatient peal of the doorbell. There stood our granddaughter, and in the gray-green eyes and impudent grin I saw the reflection of our Christmas Boy.

Behind her, lugging a large pine tree, came her mother, stepfather, and nine-year-old half brother. They swept past us in a flurry of laughter; they uncorked the sparkling cider and toasted our homecoming. Then they decorated the tree and piled gaily wrapped packages under the boughs.

"You'll recognize the ornaments," said my former daughter-in-law. "They were his. I saved them for you."

"I picked out most of the gifts, Grandma," said the nine-year-old, whom I hardly knew.

When I murmured, in remembered pain, that we

hadn't had a tree for, well, sixteen years, our cheeky grand-daughter said, "Then it's time to shape up!"

They left in a whirl, shoving one another out the door, but not before asking us to join them the next morning for church, then dinner at their home.

"Oh, we just can't," I began.

"You sure can," ordered our granddaughter, as bossy as her father had been. "I'm singing the solo, and I want to see you there."

"Bring earplugs," advised the nine-year-old.

We had long ago given up the poignant Christmas services, but now, under pressure, we sat rigid in the front pew, fighting back tears.

Then it was solo time. Our granddaughter swished (her father would have swaggered) to center stage, and the magnificent voice soared, clear and true, in perfect pitch. She sang "O Holy Night," which brought back bittersweet memories.

In a rare emotional response,

the congregation applauded in delight. How her father would have relished the moment!

We had been alerted that there would be a "whole mess of people" for dinner—but thirty-five? Assorted relatives filled every corner of the house; small children, noisy and exuberant, seemed to bounce off the walls. I could not sort out who belonged to whom, but it didn't matter. They all belonged to one another. They took us in, enfolded us in joyous camaraderie. We sang carols in loud, off-key voices, saved only by that amazing soprano.

Sometime after dinner, before the winter sunset, it occurred to me that a true family is not always one's own flesh and blood. It is a climate of the heart. Had it not been for our adopted son, we would not now be surrounded by caring strangers who would help us to hear the music again.

Later, not yet ready to give up the day, our granddaughter asked us to come along with her. "I'll drive," she said. "There's a place I like to go." She jumped behind

the wheel of the car and, with the confidence of a newly licensed driver, zoomed off toward the foothills.

Alongside the headstone rested a small, heart-shaped rock, slightly cracked, painted by our artist daughter. On its weathered surface she had written: "To my brother, with love." Across the crest of the grave lay a holly-bright Christmas wreath. Our number-two son admitted, when asked, that he sent one every year.

In the chilly but somehow comforting silence, we were not prepared for our unpredictable granddaughter's next move. Once more that day her voice, so like her father's, lifted in song, and the mountainside echoed the chorus of "Joy to the World," on and on into infinity.

When the last pure note had faded, I felt, for the first time since our son's death, a sense of peace, of the positive continuity of life, of renewed faith and hope. The real meaning of Christmas had been restored to us. Hallelujah!

Love is not blind;

love sees a great deal more

than the actual.

Love sees the ideas,

the potential in us.

OSWALD CHAMBERS

Great Lady

TIM HANSEL

remember when I was in fourth grade and you used to do things like stay up half the night just to make me a Zorro outfit for Halloween. I knew you were a good mom, but I didn't realize what a great lady you were.

I can remember your working two jobs sometimes and running the beauty shop in the front of our home so as to insure that our family would be able to make ends meet. You worked long, long hours and somehow managed to smile all the way through it. I knew you were a hard worker, but I didn't realize what a great lady you were.

I remember the night that I came to you late…in fact, it was near midnight or perhaps beyond, and told you that I was supposed to be a king in a play at school the next day. Somehow you rose to the occasion and created a king's purple robe with ermine on it (made of cotton and

black markers). After all that work I still forgot to turn around in the play, so that no one really saw the completion of all your work. Still, you were able to laugh and love and enjoy even those kinds of moments. I knew then that you were a mother like no other who could rise to any occasion, but I didn't realize what a great lady you were.

I remember when I split my head open for the sixth time in a row and you told the school, "He will be okay. Just give him a little rest. I'll come and check on him later." They knew and I knew that you were tough, but I didn't realize what a great lady you were.

I can remember in junior high and high school you helping me muddle through my homework—you making costumes for special events at school—you attending all my games. I knew at the time that you would try almost anything, if it would help one of your children, but I didn't realize what a great lady you were.

I remember bringing forty-three kids home at 3:30 one morning when I worked for Young Life and asking if it would be okay if they stayed over for the night and had breakfast. I remember you getting up at 4:30 to pull off this heroic feat. I knew at the time that you were a joyous and generous giver, but I didn't realize what a great lady you were.

I can remember you attending all my football and basketball games in high school and getting so excited that you hit the person in front of you with your pompons. I could even hear you rooting for me way out in the middle of the field. I knew then that you were one of the classic cheerleaders of all time, but I didn't realize what a great lady you were.

I remember all the sacrifices you made so I could go to Stanford—the extra work you took on, the care packages you sent so regularly, the mail that reminded me that I wasn't in this all alone. I knew you were a great friend, but I didn't realize what a great lady you were.

I remember graduating from Stanford and deciding to work for two hundred dollars a month loving kids through Young Life. Although you and Dad thought I had fallen off the end of the ladder you still encouraged me. In fact, I remember when you came down to help me fix up my little one-room abode. You added your special, loving touch to what would have been very simple

quarters. I realized then—and time and time again—what a creative genius you were, but I didn't realize what a great lady you were.

Time wore on, I grew older and got married, and started a family. You became "NaNa" and cherished your new role, yet you never seemed to grow older. I realized then that God had carved out a special place in life when he made you, but I didn't realize what a great, great lady you were.

I got slowed down by an accident. Things got a little tougher for me. But you stood alongside as you always had. Some things, I thought, never change—and I was deeply grateful. I realized then what I had known for a long time—what a great nurse you can be—but I didn't realize what a great, great lady you were.

I wrote some books, and people seemed to like them. You and Dad were so proud that sometimes you gave people copies of the books just to show what one of your kids had done. I realized then what a great promoter you

were, but I didn't realize what a great, great lady you were.

Times have changed…seasons have passed, and one of the greatest men I have ever known has passed along as well. I can still remember you at the memorial service, standing tall and proud in a brilliant purple dress, reminding people, "How blessed we have been, and how thankful we are for 'a life well lived.'" In those moments I saw a woman who could stand tall and grateful amidst the most difficult of circumstances. I was beginning to discover what a great, great lady you are.

In the last year, when you have had to stand alone as never before, all of what I have observed and experienced all those years have come together in a brand-new way. In spite of it all, now your laughter is richer, your strength is stronger, your love is deeper, and I am discovering in truth what a great, great lady you are.

Thanks for choosing me to be one of your sons.

The memory of my mother
and her teachings were,
after all, the only capital
I had to start life with,
and on that capital
I have made my way.

ANDREW JACKSON

When the Moon
Doesn't Shine

RUTH SENTER

Usually the moon shines bright on clear May nights in eastern Pennsylvania. But tonight the moon is missing. All is dark. I notice brown circles under the lamp in the hall when Mother welcomes our 2:00 A.M. arrival from Illinois. I also notice brown circles under her eyes. Spots I'd never noticed before. Tired skin under gentle folds.

But here she stands, my mother of forty years. I sense an accumulation of nights waiting up for home-coming children, as though the years have cast shadows from the lamp onto her face. I see the years in the black and blue veins that have just this week felt the heart specialist's probe. I hear the years—like the ocean ringing in a seashell—in the doctor's diagnosis. "Red flag...enlarged

heart…slow the pace…." I stare into uncertainty. Mother has been a steady pulse through the years. Tomorrow has been an assumed promise—a grand procession of family weddings, births, graduations, music recitals, ordinations, Christmas, Easter, Thanksgiving. Time has been an event, not a sequence.

As I look at Mother, I sense that someone has wound the clock. Time now has a cadence. Years have become increments. History has a beginning and an end. I shiver in the early morning chill. But then Mother's arms wrap me in warmth, and I am home. A forty-year-old child reassured by her mother's touch. There is no time in touch. Welcoming arms know not the years.

I hear the teakettle whistling. Freshly baked chocolate chip cookies wait on the old ironstone plate that once served cookies from Grandma Hollinger's kitchen. Mother's chocolate chip cookies and Grandma Hollinger's ironstone plate pull me back into timelessness. We sip peppermint tea and laugh over a silly story Dad tells.

Our laughter drowns out the clock. There is no time in laughter. Mother laughs the hardest of all. Dark circles. Tired circles of joy. Her children are home.

For a moment I forget bruised veins and ticking clocks. I am held together by things that do not change—a mother's early morning welcome, freshly baked chocolate chip cookies, an ironstone plate, peppermint tea, a mantel clock, and laughter. I am held together by a God who does not change. I know the God of time who is yet above time. I see tonight in my mother's face the strange paradox of time and timelessness. A rare glimpse of the divine.

A mother's arms are made of tenderness,

and children sleep soundly in them.

VICTOR HUGO

What Really Matters

One hundred years from now

It will not matter

What kind of car I drove,

What kind of house I lived in,

How much money I had in my bank account,

Nor what my clothes looked like.

But one hundred years from now

The world may be a little better

Because I was important

In the life of a child.

AUTHOR UNKNOWN

A MOTHER IS...

A Mother is the truest friend we have.

When trials, heavy and sudden, fall upon us;

when adversity takes the place of prosperity;

when friends who rejoice with us in our sunshine

desert us when troubles thicken around us;

still will she cling to us and endeavor,

by her kind precepts and counsels,

to dissipate the clouds of darkness

and cause peace to return to our hearts.

WASHINGTON IRVING

ACKNOWLEDGMENTS

A diligent search has been made to trace original ownership, and when necessary, permission to reprint has been obtained. If I have overlooked giving proper credit to anyone, please accept my apologies. If you will contact Multnomah Publishers, Inc., Post Office Box 1720, Sisters, Oregon 97759, correction will be made prior to additional printings. Please provide detailed information.

Acknowledgments are listed by story title in the order they appear in the book. For permission to reprint any of the stories, please request permission from the original source listed below. We appreciate the authors, publishers, and agents who granted permission for reprinting these stories.

"I Found You There" by Kathi Kingma. Used by permission of the author.

"A Mother's Letter to a Son Starting Kindergarten" by Rebecca Christian, © 1997. Used by permission of the author. All rights reserved.

"Twice Blessed" by Kathryn Lay, © 1997. Kathryn Lay is a freelance writer living in Arlington, TX. Her writing has appeared in *Guideposts*, *Woman's World*, and *Chicken Soup for the*

"Seeing Each Other in a Different Light" by Susan Manegold, © 1998. Used by permission of the author. Originally printed in *Women's World* magazine.

"She's Seventeen" by Gloria Gaither. Excerpt taken from *Let's Make a Memory* by Gloria Gaither and Shirley Dobson, © 1983, Word Publishing, Nashville, Tennessee. All rights reserved. Used by permission.

"Heartmade Valentine" by Edwina Patterson, © 2001. Used by permission. Edwina Patterson is a speaker and author of several books. She is the founder of A Heart for the Home Ministry as well as host of her original devotionals heard daily on the radio. www.heart-for-home.org or 1-800-344-8022.

"Someday" by Charles R. Swindoll. Taken from *Come Before Winter & Share My Hope*, © 1985 by Charles R. Swindoll, Inc. Used by permission of Zondervan Publishing House.

"The Bobby Pins" by Linda Goodman, © 1997. Author/ storyteller/playwright Linda Goodman is a native of Virginia's Appalachian Mountains who has been sharing her stories around the country for ten years. She can be reached at 804.778.7456 or e-mail her at happytales@aol.com. Used by permission.

"Her Path of Love" by Clare DeLong, © 1996. Used by permission of the author. Clare has contributed articles for